GORMENGHAST

Mervyn Peake

GORMENGHAST

adapted for the stage
by John Constable

OBERON BOOKS
LONDON

First published in this adaptation in 2006 by Oberon Books Ltd
521 Caledonian Road, London N7 9RH
Tel: 020 7607 3637 / Fax: 020 7607 3629
e-mail: info@oberonbooks.com
www.oberonbooks.com

Reprinted 2011

A catalogue record for this book is available from the British
Library.

ISBN: 978-1-84002-673-3

Cover photograph by Graham Fudger

for my father
Frederick Leonard Constable
aka 'Con'

and Vicky Harbord
friend
and first *Gormenghast* company manager

'Everything returns…'

Introduction

It's gratifying how many Mervyn Peake devotees agree that the stage adaptation of *Gormenghast* caught the spirit of the original. Some are impressed that I should have even attempted to dramatise that epic trilogy. From my perspective, its very size and scope, and the impossibility of representing it literally on stage, was a positive advantage. It encouraged me to strip the story down to its dramatic spine; to highlight certain stories, sacrificing others; to portray its world, not explicitly, but as a kind of shadow-play; to evoke the beauty and horror of Gormenghast, and to celebrate the life-force that lights up those 'gloomy, cavernous halls'.

This adaptation of *Gormenghast* was commissioned by the David Glass Ensemble. The director David Glass and I had worked together on their devised show *Bozo's Dead*. David then invited me to adapt Mervyn Peake's three gothic novels for the stage. We discussed his ideas for a piece of physical theatre, combining classic melodrama with elements drawn from Kabuki and Chinese theatre.

I'd read the novels as a young man. I now reread them, without taking notes, then wrote down all the scenes that stuck in my mind, mapping out a rough narrative shape. The process of reconstructing the story from memory saved me from being overwhelmed by detail. The drama evolved its own dream-like logic of jump cuts linked by recurring motifs: like that 'Field of Stones among the clouds'. I revised this initial outline in consultation with David. I then wrote the play in about a week or, more accurately, allowed it to write itself. The dialogue echoed Peake's original language – only deconstructed and reconfigured, reinvented in a heightened form.

My play takes as its main theme what Peake calls the 'ritual of the blood', the revolt of youth against the established order. It presents a world bound by iron laws and the dead weight of tradition, encapsulated in the ritual refrain: 'No change!' This old order – personified by Gertrude, the inscrutable Countess of Groan, and Barquentine, her tyrannical Master of Ritual – is confronted by three wayward children: Steerpike, the renegade kitchen boy, who seduces and murders his way up the social ladder; the Lady Fuchsia, destroyed by her forbidden love for him; and her brother, Titus, heir to Gormenghast, who comes to embody the change that threatens its very existence. The Castle itself is represented by a chorus, a tangible, brooding presence against which Titus, Fuchsia and Steerpike, each for their own reasons, react.

The three-act structure (in performance, an interval is taken between Acts Two and Three) allowed me to get to grips with the sprawling plot and the extended time-scale, to create a coherent narrative. The epic sweep of *Titus Groan* was compressed into Act I: *The Child Inheritor*, presenting key scenes from Titus's nightmarish infancy. Act II: *The Truant Earl* and Act III: *The Flood* mine a relatively narrow vein from the second *Gormenghast* novel, exploring the young man's rites of passage and his rebellion against his preordained destiny. The final scene, in which Titus rejects his inheritance and leaves Gormenghast, was inspired by a dream sequence in *Titus Alone*.

These three acts are divided into scenes of variable length, each culminating in a dramatic reversal of fortune in the lives of the principal characters. The abrupt shifts in time and place accentuate the intensity of their emotional journeys. This is melodrama: a character appears in a new scene and portrays an intention. By the end of the scene, power has shifted.

The work has a rhythm, like a musical score. In rehearsals, David refined the score, breaking down the scenes into even smaller units. Everything was strictly choreographed to serve the theatrical illusion. Yet within this discipline, the cast had enormous freedom to explore the world of the play and discover their own characters.

In the novels, the larger-than-life characters and emotions are reflected in Gormenghast's very architecture, the crumbling grandeur of that vast, rambling castle. The play attempts something similar, juxtaposing character-driven scenes of heightened naturalism with elemental set-pieces that draw on all the resources of physical theatre. Thus Steerpike's ambition and resentment manifest in acts of physical destruction – the burning of the library; the flooding of the castle – which in turn unleash an apocalypse of death, madness and revenge. My close working relationship with David Glass gave me the confidence to fully explore this sense of inner conflicts erupting into the outer world. I could write expressionistic stage directions – such as 'Flay descends…through the labyrinthine stairways and corridors' or 'The Castle Floods' – knowing that David would rise to the challenge and come up with a simple, stylised way to realise them on stage.

David Glass's extraordinary theatrical coups, John Eacott's sampled score, Spike Mosley's atmospheric lighting, Sally Owen's choreography and, not least, the physical versatility of the cast and their willingness to take risks – all these combined to create the world of Gormenghast within designer Rae Smith's shape-shifting, minimalist set.

The original production opened at the Alhambra Studio Theatre, Bradford, in 1992, followed by a British tour which culminated at BAC. The play subsequently transferred to the Lyric, Hammersmith, where it returned for a second run. Further revivals and international British Council tours followed, to critical and popular acclaim. As I write, a new production by the David Glass Ensemble is in rehearsal.

I hope this publication of the play will inspire new generations of actors and directors to venture beyond the confines of naturalism and social realism, to realise the potential for physical theatre to tell epic stories. I'm confident that it will also show how powerfully Mervyn Peake's remote, chimerical world still resonates with our own.

J.C.
London, 2006

A note on design

The David Glass Ensemble production, designed by Rae Smith and directed by David Glass, was staged within a minimalist black-box set. Upstage: a black half-backdrop with seven doors. Above, centre: a raised rostrum, creating an upper level. Moveable black flats, bamboo poles and silks were used to create the other environments and effects. Lighting, the live music by John Eacott, and the physicality of the Ensemble were all key elements in creating the world of Gormenghast.

Characters

CHORUS
the Voices of Gormenghast

COUNTESS
Gertrude, Countess of Groan; mother of Titus

BARQUENTINE
Master of Ritual

SEPULCHRAVE
76th Earl of Groan; father of Titus

DR PRUNESQUALLOR
Physician to the House of Groan

FUCHSIA
Titus' elder sister

CORA & CLARICE
Sepulchrave's sisters; Titus' twin aunts

FLAY
ancient Retainer to the House of Groan

SWELTER
the Cook

STEERPIKE
a kitchen boy

TITUS
77th Earl of Groan; heir to Gormenghast

THE THING
an outcast wild child

THE ENSEMBLE
Grey Scrubbers, servants, guards

The action takes place over fourteen years,
in the crumbling vastness of Gormenghast Castle,
a closed, changeless world, bound by ancient rituals.

This stage adaptation of Mervyn Peake's *Gormenghast* was commissioned and first produced by the David Glass Ensemble at the Alhambra Theatre, Bradford, on 22 January 1992, with the following cast:

COUNTESS, Di Sherlock
BARQUENTINE, Paul Hamilton
SEPULCHRAVE, Peter Bailie
DR PRUNESQUALLOR, David Tysall
FUCHSIA, Hayley Carmichael
CORA & CLARICE, Di Sherlock / Hayley Carmichael
FLAY, Paul Hamilton
SWELTER, David Tysall
STEERPIKE, Richard Attlee
TITUS, Peter Bailie
THE THING, Sally O'Donnell
CHORUS, The Ensemble

Directed by David Glass
Designed by Rae Smith
Live music composed and played by John Eacott
Choreographed by Sally Owen
Lighting designer Spike Mosley

In the 1994 production at The Lyric, Hammersmith, and subsequent British Council tour, Sepulchrave and Titus were played by Ewen Bremner; Dr Prunesquallor and Swelter by Julian Bleach; Fuchsia by Stephanie Buttle; and Steerpike by Gavin Marshall. John Eacott's music was played by Sarah Collins.

Act One
The Child Inheritor

SCENE 1
Gormenghast Castle: The Voices

A gloomy, cavernous hall, pierced by a shaft of light. Muffled sounds of crumbling masonry. The pregnant COUNTESS is borne in procession upon a palanquin. The black-robed ENSEMBLE forms a CHORUS: the fragmented, whispering, echoing voices of Gormenghast.

CHORUS: Gormenghast...
     Withdrawn and ruinous... I brood in umbra...
     Shadows of time-eaten buttresses...
     Towers patched with black ivy...
     A Field of Stones amongst the stars...
     Echoing throat of owls by night...

     Stones have their voices...
     Voices that grind from the grey lungs of granite...
     Lungs of blue air and the white lungs of rivers...
     Green voice of the garden... overgrown... gone
       forever...
     Voices that he shall hear when his ear is tuned...
     To Gormenghast, whose voice is endless...

SCENE 2
Birth of Titus

The great hall fills with the flapping and shrieking of birds.
The COUNTESS cries out, panting in labour.
The CHORUS closes around her, contracting in spasms and panting like a woman in labour. Sound of a great egg cracking open. The CHORUS holds aloft the infant TITUS.

SCENE 3

No Change!

BARQUENTINE, the Master of Ritual, bangs his wooden crutch, declaiming:

BARQUENTINE: To Gormenghast, a son.

CHORUS: A Groan is born!

Ritual music. BARQUENTINE summons the key players in the ritual. They present themselves in their ceremonial roles.

BARQUENTINE: Lord Sepulchrave, seventy-sixth Earl of Groan and Lord of Gormenghast.

CHORUS: No change!

BARQUENTINE: The Lady Gertrude, Countess of Groan.

CHORUS: No change!

BARQUENTINE: To Gormenghast, a son.

CHORUS: A Groan is born. No change!

DR PRUNESQUALLOR hands the COUNTESS her baby. BARQUENTINE blows dust from an ancient tome, opens it, instructing the COUNTESS to place TITUS upon it.

BARQUENTINE: It is written, and the writing adhered to, that the first-born male child of the House of Groan be laid among the pages that are heavy with words and engulfed in the waters, as One with the inviolate Law. I, Barquentine, Master of Ritual…

COUNTESS: (*Deposits the child on the book, wearily.*) How much more?

BARQUENTINE: (*Darts a pained look at the COUNTESS, then, lowering the book to immerse it in the font.*) I place Thee, Child Inheritor, of a thousand broken turrets and walls that crumble…

TITUS falls to the floor, wails. A shocked silence, broken by DR PRUNESQUALLOR's high-pitched nervous laugh.

PRUNESQUALLOR: (*To COUNTESS.*) Hahaha! They resemble rubber, your Ladyship! Just a core of India rubber with an elastic centre. Every ounce a bounce! Hahaha! Every ounce a bounce!

COUNTESS: What are you talking about, man?

PRUNESQUALLOR: I was referring to your child, who has just fallen…

COUNTESS: Fallen?!

PRUNESQUALLOR: To earth, your Ladyship. Hahaha! Earth, that is, with a veneer of wood and carpet between it and his tiny Lordship, whom you can doubtless hear screaming…

COUNTESS: Ah! So that's what it is! (*To BARQUENTINE.*) Well?

BARQUENTINE: (*Retrieves the screaming child, plunges him in the water, intoning:*) Your name is Titus! Titus, seventy-seventh Earl of Groan and Lord of Gormenghast. I dedicate you to your father's house. Titus, to Gormenghast, be true.

ALL: Titus!

BARQUENTINE: (*Bangs his crutch to herald the departure of each.*) The Lady Gertrude, Countess of Groan… The Lady Fuchsia, bearing her brother, Lord Titus… Lord Sepulchrave shall proceed to the hollow halls to fulfil the ancient word…

Exeunt, in procession: COUNTESS, FUCHSIA, TITUS, attended by DR PRUNESQUALLOR, SEPULCHRAVE with RETAINERS, BARQUENTINE. He roars at FLAY, off.

Flay! As Retainer-in-Chief to his Lordship, you shall descend to the Great Kitchen to do the Honours with Swelter. The lice in my beard alone know, but there it is, by the black souls of the unbelievers, the Law of laws, the Rite of rites… (*Proclaiming.*) No change! (*Roaring.*) Flay!

SCENE 4
Flay's Journey To The Underworld

FLAY, the Earl's cadaverous, taciturn, stubbornly loyal servant, descends to the kitchens, travelling through the labyrinthine stairways and corridors of Gormenghast, his every step punctuated by the cracking of his knee-joints.

The ENSEMBLE create the passages and stairways with moveable black flats, to a sound collage: FLAY's cracking knee-joints and echoing footsteps; crumbling masonry, dripping water; the creaking and banging of doors.

SCENE 5
Swelter's Kitchen / Steerpike's Escape

FLAY opens the door to the Great Kitchen: an underworld of ovens and steaming cauldrons. Sound: the VOICES of hordes of GREY SCRUBBERS (kitchen boys) yelling above the infernal din with a crazed, sycophantic fervour.

SWELTER, the fat, drunken chef of Gormenghast, appears through another door, wielding a bottle of wine and a blood-splattered cleaver. FLAY observes SWELTER's debauch.

SCRUBBERS: Shall we cook it, sir? We'll do it now, sir! Slosh it in the copper, sir! Oh! What a tasty dish, sir!

SWELTER: (*Roars.*) Scrubbers! Shilence! Shilence, my fairy boys, my ghastly fillets! (*The hubbub subsides.*) I am Swelter, the chef of Gormenghast, which meansh that I am the shymbol of exchellence and plenty. Who did I shay I was?

SCRUBBERS: Swelter! Swelter, sir! Swelter!

SWELTER: Thatsh right! Thatsh right! Swelter! (*Fondles his cleaver.*) We'll make 'em turn, my dears, we'll make 'em turn, and what a turn – for them and the worms that nibble 'em! Where's Steerpike?

STEERPIKE, a moody, high-shouldered boy, steps forward to face SWELTER.

I shall shing to you, Steerpike, to you, the hideous and insidious – only to you, my core of curdled cat-bile.

(*Kisses STEERPIKE, who remains aloof.*) It is a shong, my Steerpike, to an imaginawary monshter jusht like yourshelf, if only you were a twifle bigger and more monshtrous still. (*Swigs from bottle.*)

> (*Sings.*) I am the chef Shwelter, I wallow and welter
> In blood, gutsh and greash from my neck to my knees,
> Cook to his Lordshipsh, wardshipsh, and all shouls
>   aboardshipsh
> That shail on shlippery sheas...

Whasha matter, Steerpike? You doeshn't like my shinging? And what do you proposhe to do in thish batter? I've sheen you! I've sheen you looking at me with your insholent animal eyes. You're looking at me now. Tell me, Shteerpike, what doesh it all mean?

Enraged by his refusal to react, SWELTER raises his cleaver to strike STEERPIKE, but suddenly sags, crumples and collapses in a drunken stupor.
STEERPIKE regards the snoring lump with contempt. At the sound of FLAY's cracking joints, he skulks into the shadows.
FLAY approaches the supine chef, kicks him.

(*Groans and sits up, rubbing his eyes.*) Well, well, well! Baste me to a frazzle it if isn't Mister Flay!

FLAY: (*Commanding.*) Up! Honours! (*SWELTER lumbers to his feet.*) A Groan is born! (*Performs ritual signs.*) No change!

SWELTER: (*Retches, vomits, then, wiping his mouth:*) Thatsh better!

FLAY strikes SWELTER with his bunch of keys, then strides off in disgust. STEERPIKE slips out of the shadows to follow him. SWELTER rubs his face.

(*With a ghastly grin.*) Revengsh (*Fondles the cleaver.*) I'll make you red and wet, my pretty. Oh! so red and wet! Revengsh!

Lights fade on kitchen. STEERPIKE shadows FLAY along stone corridors lit by guttering candles.
FLAY ducks into an alcove, ambushing him.

FLAY: What's this? Grey Scrubber. One of Swelter's rats, eh? Lost in the Stone Lanes? What do you want, Swelter's boy?

STEERPIKE: (*Cringing.*) Vile Swelter... Nauseating Swelter...

FLAY: H'm. Name?

STEERPIKE: Steerpike, sir.

FLAY: Queerpike? Eh? Eh?

STEERPIKE: Steerpike! Steerpike!

FLAY: Two Squeertikes. H'm. Wait here.

SCENE 6

The Countess Gertrude

Below: FLAY takes a bunch of keys, unlocks a rusty iron door, enters a secret passage and uncovers a spyhole. He signals to STEERPIKE, who creeps over to peer through it.
Lights up on what he sees:
Above: the Countess's bedroom – candlelit, shambolic, alive with birdsong, the cawing of crows. The COUNTESS is in bed, dreamily stroking a raven perched on her hand.

COUNTESS: (*To raven.*) What a bunch of feathered wickedness! What clouds has he been flying through? Oh? So you beg my pardon, do you – a great treeful of forgiveness?

She gives a low whistle. White cats glide into the room, padding and purring around her.

STEERPIKE: (*Spying on the COUNTESS, whispers:*) The cats and birds, sir – who do they belong to?

FLAY: Belong to my Lady...

STEERPIKE: The Countess Gertrude? That old bunch of rags!

FLAY: Shhh! Swelter's boy! (*They resume spying.*)

Cats commence an eerie yowling.

COUNTESS: (*Sings.*) Around the shores of the Elegant Isles
  Where the cat-fish bask and purr
  And lick their paws with adhesive smiles
  And wriggle their fins of fur.
  And the flying-fish feathers fall...

Her singing trails off at the appearance of FUCHSIA and DR PRUNE-SQUALLOR, who solemnly presents her with the baby Titus. She stares at the child distractedly.

Well? What do you want me to do with him?

PRUNESQUALLOR: Do? My Lady, by all that's maternal... Hahahaha! I never order – haha – oh no! I merely advise...

COUNTESS: Take it away, 'Squallor. Find a wet nurse from among the Mud Dwellers. Here is the Key which may not be used. Let him wear it on a chain around his neck.

She gives him the Key. They make ritual gestures.

I would like to see the boy when he is... six!

FUCHSIA: (*Bursting into tears.*) Oh, how I hate, hate, hate! How I hate people!

PRUNESQUALLOR: Fuchsia, my dear child! What's wrong?

FUCHSIA: Everything's wrong! Everything! I shall live alone, in a tree or a tower. Someone will come then, from a new world, someone who is different, who'll love me for what I am!

FUCHSIA runs off, DR PRUNESQUALLOR trailing ineffectually after her.
FLAY closes the peephole, blacking out the Countess's room.

STEERPIKE: (*Whistles.*) That was the Lady Fuchsia?

FLAY: Enough, Swelter's boy! Back to your kitchen.

STEERPIKE: Back to that hideous cook? Oh no!

FLAY draws himself up in amazement at the boy's insolence.

If you send me back to Swelter, I'll tell him about your spyhole. I'll tell him all about the Lady Fuchsia.

FLAY: What? Come here! Been a-gaping, have you? A-gaping and a-listening? I'll fix you. I'll break your bones!

FLAY propels STEERPIKE down the passage, unlocks a cell, pushes him inside and locks the door.

H'm… my fault… Shouldn't have… Saw too much… H'm…

Exit FLAY, muttering to himself.

SCENE 7
Steerpike's Journey / The Field of Stones

STEERPIKE broods in his prison cell. He lopes around the room, looking for a means of escape. He leans out of the only window, gazing down and almost fainting with vertigo. He crawls through the opening and begins scaling the sheer wall, scrabbling for chinks in the stone, clinging to strands of ivy. He loses his grip, clutching and swinging on a creeper. He finally hauls himself up over the parapet, panting and shaking violently, to collapse on the roof. Night falls. Owls hoot. Their eyes glow in the dark. STEERPIKE wakes, shivering. He gazes out over the battlements, awe-struck, whispers:

STEERPIKE: Gormenghast!

He freezes, listening.

SCENE 8
Fuchsia

Music. A light comes on in FUCHSIA's attic below the parapet. FUCHSIA sits alone, singing a plaintive chanson.

FUCHSIA: (*Sings.*) A freckled and frivolous cake there was
      Adrift on a pointless sea,
      And a steeling knife in her wake there was
      Hell-bent on cutting her free… Her free…
      Hell-bent on cutting her free…

No one knows where I go. I go here. And here I am now.
I am Lady Fuchsia Groan. I am looking out of a window
and when I'm older I shall look out again… The same
window… Over and over again…

(*Sings.*) They fly and fly neath the lilac sky –
The frivolous cake and the knife
Who winketh his glamorous indigo eye
At the crumbs of his future wife… His wife…
The crumbs of his future…

*STEERPIKE bursts in through the window. FUCHSIA
screams, backing off in terror.*

Who are you? What are you doing here? This is my room,
my secret, mine! No one else knows! How did you find it?
Where do you come from? What do you want?

*STEERPIKE allows her to finish her outburst before speaking,
slowly, mystically.*

STEERPIKE: Tonight, I saw a great field of stones among the
clouds. A world where no one has been for hundreds of
years. One day I should like to take you there.

FUCHSIA: How dare you! How dare you! How did you get
here?

STEERPIKE: Escaped… climbing… all night… cold…
hungry…

FUCHSIA: (*Warily.*) Are you an adventurer?

STEERPIKE: Lady Fuchsia I come to you for sanctuary. I am
at your service as a dreamer and a man of action. (*Bows.*)

FUCHSIA: No, no – you can't stay here! You mustn't! Go
away!

STEERPIKE: Where can I go? Lady Fuchsia, I am a man
of purpose. Help me! Introduce me to someone who will
employ me.

FUCHSIA: And you'll go away, and never breathe a word to
anyone… Promise?

STEERPIKE nods eagerly.

Well... there's my Aunts, Cora and Clarice – they're always complaining they haven't got a servant. But I warn you, they're both quite mad.

STEERPIKE: Leave them to me.

A knock at the door. They freeze.

Lady Fuchsia, I am a rebel, a renegade. Will you betray me?

PRUNESQUALLOR: (*Knocking, off.*) Fuchsia! Are you all right, child?

FUCHSIA: (*Hesitates, staring wildly at STEERPIKE, then takes the plunge, calling out.*) It's all right, Doctor Prune. I'm going to visit my Aunts... (*To STEERPIKE, hissing defiantly.*) There!

They freeze, startled by the sound of:

SCENE 9
The Thing

THE THING, a half-naked, mud-smeared wild child, wakes in her bed of leaves and flowers. She stretches and shakes, unleashing the sounds of the wild: shrill birds; primeval shrieks and roars. Her cries echo throughout the Castle.

SCENE 10
Sepulchrave's Library

A door slams, shutting out the cries of THE THING.
The library. SEPULCHRAVE is on his throne, sunk in a deep depression. He stares blankly at FLAY, who places an open book in his hands. The old Earl's spirits revive as he turns the pages, utterly entranced. The books in his library seem to flap and fly around him. Distance hooting of owls.

SEPULCHRAVE: (*Slaps the book shut.*) Flay! (*FLAY bows.*) I want to see my son. My son, Flay, heir to Gormenghast... Without Titus the castle has no future when I am gone.

FLAY: No change, Lordship.

SEPULCHRAVE: I have decided on a family gathering here
in the library. You will inform the Countess, Fuchsia, Cora
and Clarice... Have Doctor Prunesquallor bring Titus.
(*Hands him invitation cards.*)

FLAY: Barquentine, Lordship?

SEPULCHRAVE: (*Sighs.*) Yes, yes... My Master of Ritual...
(*Makes an absent gesture of dismissal.*)

*FLAY leaves the library. SEPULCHRAVE stares distractedly
at the book in his lap. Owls hoot.*

SCENE 11
Swelter Sharpens His Cleaver

*FLAY walks across an empty courtyard, muttering to himself,
accompanied by the retorts of his knee-joints. He stops dead,
listening to the sound of grinding metal. He traces the sound to
a window, creeps up and peers through it, sees:
The kitchen lit by flashes of lime-green light. SWELTER is
sharpening his cleaver on a grindstone, testing the blade. He places
a cake on the floor, addressing it as 'Mr Flay'. Then, tip-toeing
up on the cake, he strikes, splitting it clean in two. He gurgles
grotesquely, fondling the cleaver.
FLAY recoils, catching his breath.*

SCENE 12
Cora and Clarice

*FLAY walks along a corridor, slowly recovering his composure.
He knocks at a door. STEERPIKE opens it.*

STEERPIKE: Well, well, well! Baste me to a frazzle, if it isn't
Mr Flay!

FLAY: H'm... Swelter's boy.

STEERPIKE: No more, sir. I am presently engaged as
personal valet to the ladies Cora and Clarice.

FLAY: H'm… (*Thrusts card at him.*) Invitation.

FLAY shuffles off, muttering to himself.

CORA / CLARICE: Who is it, Steerpike? Who is it?

STEERPIKE: (*Plays with the card then, making a snap decision, hides it.*) Your Ladyships, this is too much! (*They stare at him blankly.*) Everyone knows how the Countess Gertrude stole what is rightfully yours.

CLARICE: Yes! Yes! Our birds!

CORA: He's talking about our power, dear.

CLARICE: No! It's power we want. Lots of power!

STEERPIKE: But this latest scandal… Below stairs they speak of nothing else. 'They haven't been asked.' – they say – 'They haven't been asked!'

CLARICE: Asked what?

CORA: Asked where?

STEERPIKE: To the Great Gathering which your brother has called to honour your nephew Titus. Everybody who is anybody will be there. Even Prunesquallor's invited.

CORA / CLARICE: Gertrude! This is her doing!

STEERPIKE: Your Ladyships, answer me, do you believe in honour?

They glance at one another, nodding mechanically.

Do you believe that injustice should dominate the Castle?

They shake their heads.

Do you believe that it should flourish without retribution?

They hesitate, shaking their heads uncertainly.

Then tell me – who controls Gormenghast? Who allows the great traditions to fall into neglect? Who forgets even his own blood and lineage? Who is that man?

CORA / CLARICE: Gertrude! Gertrude!

STEERPIKE: Come, come! Who is 'that man' who forgets even his own sisters?

CORA / CLARICE: Sepulchrave? Sepulchrave!

STEERPIKE: Lord Sepulchrave. If I am to restore your rights, we have to reckon with your selfish brother.

CORA / CLARICE: (*Whispering.*) What must we do? Tell us what to do! Tell us!

STEERPIKE: There must be no half-measures. It's all or nothing!

CORA / CLARICE: All or nothing! All or nothing!

STEERPIKE whispers in their ears. They work themselves into a frenzy, crying in flat expressionless voices.

Burn? Burn. Burn! Burn! Burn!

STEERPIKE: Silence! Both of you! Sit down!

They sit obediently, the life draining out of them.

Who is it who will raise you to your golden thrones?

CORA / CLARICE: Thrones… Our thrones… Golden ones. That's what we want!

STEERPIKE: Who is it who will raise you?

CORA / CLARICE: Steerpike. Steerpike will raise us. Then we'll have power. We will, won't we?

STEERPIKE: Your Ladyships will then have power.

CORA / CLARICE: Burn. Burn. Burn! Burn! Burn!

SCENE 13
The Burning Books

The Library. SEPULCHRAVE enthroned. Enter, in procession: BARQUENTINE, DR PRUNESQUALLOR, bearing TITUS (doll), COUNTESS (with cat) and FUCHSIA. They pay homage to SEPULCHRAVE, taking their places.

SEPULCHRAVE: (*Reaching out for TITUS.*) My son…

BARQUENTINE: (*Bangs his crutch, calling SEPULCHRAVE to order.*) We are gathered together in this ancient library at the instigation of Sepulchrave, seventy-sixth Earl of Groan…

SEPULCHRAVE: (*Insistently.*) My son!

BARQUENTINE: As Master of Ritual, I confirm that for his Lordship to call for his son in no way contravenes the tenets of Gormenghast…

SEPULCHRAVE: For God's sake!

BARQUENTINE: But your Lordship, it is to this child… (*Coughs.*)

COUNTESS: (*Stroking her mewing cat.*) Are you hungry, my love?

BARQUENTINE: (*Irritably.*) It is to Lord Titus… (*Signals to PRUNESQUALLOR who walks Titus forward.*) I will turn my back on you and strike the earth four times… (*Coughs.*) Whereupon the Countess… (*Coughs.*)

FLAY, FUCHSIA and DR PRUNESQUALLOR sniff the air, coughing, as smoke fills the room.

Whereupon… (*Has a violent fit of coughing.*)

COUNTESS: What is the matter, man?

PRUNESQUALLOR: The matter, as far as I dare to judge at such very short notice, is a case of thickening atmosphere – hahaha!

FUCHSIA: Quick! (*Runs to the door.*) It's locked!

ALL: Locked?

PRUNESQUALLOR: By all that's perfidious, this is most intriguing. Perhaps a bit too intriguing, eh Fuchsia? Can we breach it, your Lordship? Can it be smashed?

SEPULCHRAVE: Too thick, Prunesquallor... four-inch oak...

The cat mews, breaking free of the COUNTESS's embrace, and escapes. The fire is enacted in a sequence of melodramatic tableaux, punctuated by the following lines:

BARQUENTINE: Hell-fire, treachery!

FUCHSIA: (*Shouting.*) Fire! Help! Fire! Help! Fire! Fire!

SEPULCHRAVE: My books! My books!

FUCHSIA: Where's Titus?

PRUNESQUALLOR: Oh! I've got him! Hahaha!

COUNTESS: Prunesquallor! Have you seen the cat?

PRUNESQUALLOR: Damn the cat, madam, and all its furred and feathered friends!

COUNTESS, outraged, punches DR PRUNESQUALLOR. SEPULCHRAVE stands in their midst, gazing transfixed at his burning library. Sound of breaking glass.

STEERPIKE: Hold on! I'm letting down a ladder! Don't panic! The Heir of Gormenghast, where is he? Where's Lord Titus?

FUCHSIA: Here! (*Passes Titus up to STEERPIKE.*)

COUNTESS: Fuchsia!

FUCHSIA: No, mother. You first!

COUNTESS: Do as you're told, child!

STEERPIKE helps FUCHSIA and COUNTESS climb out.

STEERPIKE: (*To SEPULCHRAVE.*) Your Lordship.

SEPULCHRAVE: (*Helped up the ladder by STEERPIKE and PRUNESQUALLOR.*) I am sorry to have kept you...

BARQUENTINE and DR PRUNESQUALLOR scramble out. Sound of the burning roof caving in. The survivors reappear one by one, gathering outside the blazing library. The first to emerge is STEERPIKE, carrying Titus, leading FUCHSIA.

FUCHSIA: Steerpike…

STEERPIKE silences her with a look, indicating the COUNTESS, who reappears clutching her precious cat. FLAY follows, trying to attract her attention.

FLAY: My Lady… Lord Sepulchrave…

ALL stare as SEPULCHRAVE enters, hollow-eyed, moving like a somnambulist. An owl hoots.

FUCHSIA: (*Runs to embrace SEPULCHRAVE.*) Father! Oh, father! What is it?

SEPULCHRAVE: (*Staring vacantly.*) I am not your father. I live in the Field of Stones.
I am the Death Owl! (*His fingers curl. He hoots like an owl.*)

PRUNESQUALLOR: Come, child. (*Leads FUCHSIA away.*)

STEERPIKE pulls a face, mocking SEPULCHRAVE's madness. FLAY, enraged, seizes the COUNTESS's cat and hurls it at him. ALL freeze in shock. STEERPIKE sycophantically returns the cat to her.
The COUNTESS stares at FLAY, momentarily speechless with fury. FLAY bows his head, awaiting his fate.

COUNTESS: Fool! You are no more! Gormenghast is finished with you.
Out! Out! The castle spews you!

The COUNTESS strides off, followed by her retinue. BARQUENTINE ushers out the distracted SEPULCHRAVE. Owls hoot. FLAY is left alone, outcast, abandoned. He makes to leave – then stops dead, hearing the high-pitched whine of a grindstone.

SCENE 14
Swelter's Death

Flashes of lime-green light on SWELTER in his kitchen, sharpening his cleaver. FLAY stalks the sound. He stops, disturbed by the loud cracking sounds of his own knee-joints. He hurries off.
SWELTER appears, creeping on tip-toe, stalking FLAY.
FLAY re-appears, his knees wrapped in bandages, silently stalking SWELTER. He tries a few tentative steps, adjusts the bandages, tries again. Having satisfied himself that he can move in absolute silence, he creeps up behind SWELTER. He springs forward, lunging with his sword. SWELTER wheels around, swinging his cleaver. He gurgles with pleasure at the prospect of Flay's decapitation, then, at the sight of him still alive, bellows with rage. They fight like two primeval monsters. SWELTER gains the upper hand, driving FLAY back. FLAY, dodging the slashing cleaver, trips and falls. SWELTER towers over him, grunting and drooling.

SWELTER: Goodbye, Mr Flay.

He examines his cleaver, then, clutching it in both hands, raises it above his head to strike. As he looks up, he freezes, staring up at SEPULCHRAVE.
Above: SEPULCHRAVE perched on the roof, staring down at them. He hoots like an owl.
FLAY plunges his sword into SWELTER's vast belly. SWELTER pulls out his own guts, staring at them in astonishment, then totters and falls stone dead.
SEPULCHRAVE is transformed into an owl with glowing saucer-eyes. He hoots, ordering FLAY to pass the entrails up to him. FLAY obeys, horrified, offering up the entrails on his sword.
The screech of the Death Owl echoes through the smoking ruins of Gormenghast.

Act Two
The Truant Earl

SCENE 1
Child Titus

TITUS, a sensitive, withdrawn seven year-old boy, clutches his doll, hearing a CHORUS of mocking CHILDREN.

CHORUS: Titus Groan, scrag and bone,
      Father vanished in the Field of Stone.
      Field in the clouds where his Lordship's cook
      Got fed to an owl with a beak like a hook.
      Found no body so they dug no grave.
      Some say the owl was Sepulchrave.

TITUS transfixed among the black-robed CHORUS of whispering GHOSTS and PHANTOMS.

      Titus the seventy-seventh…
      Earl and Master of Gormenghast…
      Heir to a craggy ruin…
      Sea of nettles… Empire of red rust…
      Titus the child suckled on shadows…
      Weaned on webs of ritual… Labyrinth of stone…
      And eyes… Eyes to watch and feet to follow…
      And hands… Hands to hold fast and guide him…

CHORUS manipulates TITUS like a puppet.
The COUNTESS and FUCHSIA appear in the distance, moving like sleepwalkers.

      His mother, the Countess, half-asleep, half-aware…
      A furlong of white cats trail after her…
      Sister Fuchsia, sullen, tender, suspicious, credulous…
      Barquentine, the foul Master of Ritual…

Enter BARQUENTINE, Master of Ritual. He has a lame leg, yet moves with remarkable agility. He bangs his crutch. The CHORUS disperses. STEERPIKE slips out of the shadows, catching his eye.

SCENE 2

Barquentine's Apprentice

BARQUENTINE: (*Summoning STEERPIKE.*) Ferret! Yes you – bastard whelp of a whore rat! Tell me, ferret, how old is Lord Titus?

STEERPIKE: Seven, sir.

BARQUENTINE: Ferret, your answer's good.

BARQUENTINE blows dust from an ancient tome, thrusts it at STEERPIKE.

And what is this, boy?

STEERPIKE: It is the Law, sir.

BARQUENTINE: By the blind powers, it's the truth. (*Whacks him with the book, knocking him down.*) And what is Law? Answer me, curse you! (*Kicks him.*)

STEERPIKE: Destiny, sir. Destiny.

BARQUENTINE: Body of me, Destiny it is. What's your bastard name, boy?

STEERPIKE: Steerpike, sir.

BARQUENTINE: Age?

STEERPIKE: Seventeen.

BARQUENTINE: Seventeen! Bloody wrinkles! So they still spawn 'em so! Who's your master?

STEERPIKE: (*Considers.*) I have no immediate master. I try to make myself useful here and there.

BARQUENTINE: 'Here and there.' By the stones, you don't fool me! I see through you, suckling, bones and brain! You're a neat little rat, but there'll be no more 'here and there' for you. You'll make yourself useful 'here', to me! Understand?

STEERPIKE: What's in it for me, sir?

BARQUENTINE: Your keep, you insolent bastard! Your keep! Hell-fire, have you no pride? A roof, your food and the honour of studying the Ritual, the secrets of the Groans. Body of me, I have no son – you must learn the Iron Trade. Are you ready?

STEERPIKE: Never more so.

BARQUENTINE: Slimebag! (*Summoning TITUS.*) Groan! Titus Groan.

TITUS steps forward nervously.

'It is written and the writing adhered to… ' (*On an impulse, placing the book in STEERPIKE's hands.*) Read, weasel!

STEERPIKE takes the book, glancing at TITUS.

STEERPIKE: (*Reads from book.*) '… That on the seventh day of the seventh month of his seventh year, the seventy-seventh Earl shall cast a golden coil upon the waters of the moat to sink into the reflection of his mother's face in a tower window… '

SCENE 3
Passage of Time

Ritual music. CHORUS descends on TITUS, guiding him through the various ritual motions. BARQUENTINE and STEERPIKE's voices overlap as they traverse seven years.

BARQUENTINE: '… That on the sixth day of the third month of his ninth year, Lord Titus shall release a magpie from a cage… '

STEERPIKE: '… That on the fourteenth day of the fifth month of his tenth year, he shall carve a crescent moon… '

BARQUENTINE: '… That on the third day of the seventh month of his eleventh year, he shall unlock the Tower of Flints… '

STEERPIKE: '... That on the second Sunday of the tenth month of his twelfth year, he shall stand when the rest are seated and seat himself when the rest are standing... '

BARQUENTINE: '... That on the twenty-third day of the seventh month of his thirteenth year, clasping in his left hand a beaker of moat-water in which the Countess shall place the blue pebble from Gormenghast River... '

CHORUS withdraws. Ritual music fades as STEERPIKE steps forward to blindfold the fourteen year-old TITUS.

STEERPIKE: '... That on the morning of his fourteenth birthday, he shall be led blindfold to the shores of the Great Lake, clasping in his right hand the Key that may not be used.'

TITUS: (*Struggling ineffectually.*) No! Why should I?

STEERPIKE: Nothing to do with me, your Lordship. It's the Law.

TITUS: The Law, the Law – I hate the Law!

STEERPIKE: 'He shall remain in darkness until the stroke of twelve... '

STEERPIKE withdraws, leaving TITUS alone, blindfolded.

SCENE 4
The Garden

THE THING appears. She circles the blindfolded TITUS warily, sniffing the air, unable to resist her curiosity.

TITUS: (*To himself.*) So! I'm Lord of Gormenghast am I? Then why do I have to report to Steerpike to do these stupid rituals? They give you the key to the castle gate, then tell you you can't use it. What's the use of a key if it doesn't unlock a door? It's a rotten trick!

THE THING suddenly hurls herself on TITUS, ripping off the blindfold. They freeze. TITUS laughs, delighted with what he sees, trying to reassure her. THE THING plays with him,

then takes flight, floating effortlessly away. TITUS gives chase. She leads him through ruined halls, dancing tantalisingly out of reach. TITUS chases her off.
THE THING reappears, alone, in an overgrown garden, rejoicing in her freedom. Taking up a bamboo pole, she uses it to disturb the green canopy, releasing a riot of twittering birds.
TITUS bursts in, startling her. THE THING attacks, knocking him over, then vanishes into the undergrowth.
TITUS picks himself up, catching his breath, listening: birdsong; the drone of bees.

The Garden! They say it doesn't exist, but I found it. It's mine! (*Calling out.*) Where are you?

Sound of cracking twigs. TITUS is rooted to the spot, suddenly terrified. FLAY emerges from the bushes. He stops dead, staring at TITUS, amazed.

Who are you?

FLAY: Flay...

TITUS: Flay! I've heard of you.

FLAY: Aye... likely enough, my Lord.

TITUS: They told me you were dead, Mr Flay.

FLAY: Good as, Lordship. Banished. When your father... You were only... What you doing here, my Lord?

TITUS: I escaped, Mr Flay – ran away...

FLAY: Escaped? Ran away from the Castle? No, no... mustn't do that. Must send you back...

TITUS: I saw it, Mr Flay, I saw it!

FLAY: Saw what, Lordship?

TITUS: The Thing... A flying thing... She led me to the garden... Is she real? Have you seen her? Who is she, Mr Flay?

A pool of light, left, reveals a white cat with a raven in its mouth. Enter COUNTESS, horrified by what she sees.

34

COUNTESS: Hold! Drop it!

The cat drops the raven at her feet and slinks off. The COUNTESS picks up the raven, nursing it.

There, there... (*Broods.*) Cat hunting bird – now there's an omen! What does it mean? 'A raven's blood foretells the flood...'

TITUS, FLAY and COUNTESS, isolated in three pools of light. TITUS's conversation with FLAY is intercut with the COUNTESS's speech to the raven.

TITUS: Mr Flay... Is it true my mother banished you?

FLAY: Aye... Countess... How is she, Lordship?

TITUS: I don't know. I don't see much of her.

FLAY: Ah... a fine, proud woman. She understands the evil and the glory.

COUNTESS: (*Lowers her voice, speaking urgently to raven.*) Listen... Things are bad. There's evil afoot. I know it... (*Fiercely.*) Let 'em try! We'll hold our horses. Let 'em rear their ugly heads!

FLAY: Follow her, my Lord. Do your ancient duty and Gormenghast will be well.

TITUS: But I don't want any duties. I want to be free!

FLAY: A wicked thing to say, my Lord, a wicked thing. You are a Groan of the blood – last of the line.

COUNTESS: In Titus it's all rooted – stone and mountain, the blood and the observance. Let 'em touch him! For every hair that's hurt I'll stop a heart! (*Storms off.*)

FLAY: (*To TITUS.*) You must not fail the Stones!

Sound of a slamming door, echoing. Lights snap out.

SCENE 5

Steerpike Visits The Aunts

STEERPIKE moves stealthily through a maze of passageways to a deserted lane in a remote part of the castle. He unlocks a cell-door.

STEERPIKE: (*Calling into the cell.*) How are my lovebirds?

CORA and CLARICE burst out, jabbering:

CORA / CLARICE: Where have you been? We thought you'd forgotten us. It's been years! Years! Where are our thrones? You promised us thrones. Golden ones…

STEERPIKE: Ladies, ladies! Thrones of hammered gold cannot be wrought overnight. Do you want your glory ruined by a ridiculous pair of makeshift yellow sit-upons? Do you want to be made a laughing-stock? (*They shake their heads contritely.*) Then you must leave it to me. Meanwhile, please try to preserve all dignity and silent power in your twin bosoms.

CORA: Yes! Yes! We'll preserve it in our bosoms, won't we Clarice? Our silent power.

CLARICE: Yes, all the power we've got. But we haven't got much.

STEERPIKE: When the hour comes, we will strike.

CORA / CLARICE: But what if Gertrude finds out? About the fire? (*In sudden panic, pointing at STEERPIKE.*) It's his fault, he made us do it. He made us burn the books. Dear Sepulchrave's books!

STEERPIKE: Silence! No one will find out.

They sniff.

There is no one left to find out.

They sniff again.

Have I not told you of the deadly Weasel Plague that is ravaging the Castle?

They stare at him, suddenly afraid.

Your enemies are dead.

CORA / CLARICE: Dead? Gertrude? Sepulchrave?

STEERPIKE: Titus, Fuchsia, all dead.

They stare at him stunned.

CORA / CLARICE: Dead! (*They scream.*)

STEERPIKE: Silence! You think it's easy for me to keep the plague from your door and be at your beck and call? Do you?

They shake their heads, ashamed.

Then have the grace not to interrogate me! How dare you snap at the hand that feeds you! How dare you!

He points at the cell. CORA and CLARICE shuffle back towards the door, heads bowed, moving together, looking back to make sure they're doing what's expected of them. STEERPIKE points to the ground. They obediently get down on their knees and crawl into the cell. STEERPIKE slams the door behind them, locking it.

CORA / CLARICE: (*From within, hammering on the door.*) Steerpike! Steerpike! Don't go! Don't leave us! We're frightened! Frightened!

STEERPIKE: By the blood of Barquentine, the hags must die!

SCENE 6
In the Quad

A school-bell clangs. STEERPIKE sees FUCHSIA crossing the school quadrangle below. He intercepts her.

STEERPIKE: Lady Fuchsia Groan? His Infernal Slyness, the Arch Fluke Steerpike at your service. (*Bows.*)

FUCHSIA: You shouldn't talk like that. It's not respectful.

STEERPIKE: Sometimes I have a disrespectful nature. Equality is the great thing, don't you agree Lady Fuchsia?

FUCHSIA: I don't know and I don't care.

STEERPIKE: But don't you think it's wrong that the Grey Scrubbers have to lick fat and grease from the kitchen floor while your family throw away enough food to feed them all?

FUCHSIA: I don't know. Things ought to be fair, I suppose, but I don't know anything about –

STEERPIKE: But you do! Why aren't things fair? Because of greed and cruelty and lust for power. That sort of thing must be stopped.

FUCHSIA: Why don't you stop it then?

STEERPIKE: I will.

FUCHSIA: Stop cruelty? Oh no! You're very clever, but, oh no, you couldn't do that. (*Pause, shyly.*) I remember when you climbed into my attic.

STEERPIKE: When I climbed down from the Field of Stones. One day, Lady Fuchsia, I would like to show you the roof of this great house of yours, where the owls roost. (*Takes her hand.*) Will you explore the Field of Stones with me? Will you?

FUCHSIA: (*Slaps him, then, abruptly, kisses him.*) Yes… I will…

TITUS bursts into the courtyard. He stops dead, seeing FUCHSIA with STEERPIKE.

TITUS: Fuchsia!

FUCHSIA: (*Flustered and covering up.*) Titus, where have you been? You missed the ceremony.

STEERPIKE: My Lord… (*Bows.*) By the powers vested in me, I must pronounce your Lordship's ritual penance. (*Ritually pronouncing.*) 'It is written – and the writing adhered to

– that, howsoever an Earl of Groan shall wilfully neglect his ritual obligations – that the said truant Earl – '

TITUS: (*Pointedly ignoring STEERPIKE, to FUCHSIA.*) I hate him.

FUCHSIA: Titus, that's not fair! He can't help giving you your rituals. It's not his fault. It's the Law. Father had to do it when he was alive, and his father – they all had to –

TITUS: I hate him.

FUCHSIA: Why? What's the good of hating him? You don't expect him to make an exception for you – after thousands of years. I suppose you'd rather have Barquentine. Titus my darling, you know I love you, but you're unfair. Unfair!

TITUS: I hate him. I hate the cheap and stinking guts of him!

STEERPIKE: (*Coughs politely, resuming.*) 'The said truant Earl of Groan shall crawl upon his hands and knees to the Tower of Flints, ascending by the –'

TITUS: No! I won't! Why should I take orders from you?

STEERPIKE: It's not my fault, my Lord. It's the Law. Barquentine –

TITUS: If Barquentine wants me to do his stupid penance, let him come and tell me himself. You're not Master of Ritual.

He storms off, pursued by a distraught FUCHSIA.

STEERPIKE: (*Smiles to himself.*) Not yet, my Lord... Not yet...

SCENE 7
The Murder of Barquentine

BARQUENTINE hobbles on, cursing under his breath.
STEERPIKE shadows him, mimicking his crippled gait.

BARQUENTINE: By the pox, the slippery pup was under orders to remain! By hell, there's perfidy somewhere! A substitute, hell, crap me! (*Turns sharply, catching sight of STEERPIKE, snarls.*)

STEERPIKE: Good morning, sir.

BARQUENTINE: To hell with your 'good mornings', shit-snout! You shine like a bloody land-eel. What d'you do to yourself, eh?

STEERPIKE: I suppose it's this habit of washing I seem to have got into, sir.

BARQUENTINE: Washing? I'll give you washing, you wire worm. What do you think you are, Master Steerpike? A lily? Get the shine off you.

STEERPIKE: Quite so, sir. I am too visible.

BARQUENTINE: Not when you're wanted. You can be invisible enough when you want to be, eh? Hags' hell, boy, you can be nowhere when it suits you, eh? By the guts of the great auk, I see through you, maggot! I see through you!

STEERPIKE: What, when I'm invisible, sir?

BARQUENTINE: By the piss of Satan, pug, your sauce is dangerous! Scram!

BARQUENTINE lunges at STEERPIKE who beats a hasty retreat. BARQUENTINE enters his hovel, lights a candle, squats in his chair, opens an ancient tome, blows off the dust, coughs, hawks, spits, tries to read but is unable to concentrate. STEERPIKE reappears, silently watching him.

(*Muttering.*) It has gone on long enough – too long. By the blood of hags, he knows the inner secrets. He'll have the Keys off me with his bloody efficiency…

BARQUENTINE shifts in his chair, scratching his crotch, buttocks and belly. STEERPIKE creeps up until he stands directly behind him. His shadow dances on the wall. He silently draws the sword from his sword-stick, raising it until the point is poised above his victim's ear.

(*Grumbling to himself.*) Gripes my heart! No Earl but a brat! The Countess, cat mad! And for me, no son but this upstart bastard of a Steerpike!

STEERPIKE jabs the sword into his neck. BARQUENTINE drops his crutch. His body stiffens, his mouth gaping in a silent scream. He falls in a heap, then seizes his crutch and staggers upright, his face livid with hatred.

Traitor!

STEERPIKE advances with his sword. BARQUENTINE lashes out with his crutch, knocking him down. STEERPIKE seizes a candle, setting fire to his hair and rotten rags. BARQUENTINE, ablaze and in mortal agony, catches hold of STEERPIKE's leg and hauls himself up his body to grip him tightly around the waist. STEERPIKE struggles to wrench himself free from the fiery death-grip, his own clothing catching fire. He drags himself across the room and throws himself out of the window, plunging down into the stagnant waters of the moat, with BARQUENTINE still clinging to him. He pushes the head underwater, drowning him. He surfaces, retching and choking, before passing out.
The ENSEMBLE bear STEERPIKE's body to the sick-room.

SCENE 8
The Hospital

DR PRUNESQUALLOR takes STEERPIKE's pulse, mops his brow. STEERPIKE's face and arms are raw with burns.

STEERPIKE: (*Apparently crying out in delirium.*) I tried... O Master... I tried to save you... I tried... I tried...

PRUNESQUALLOR: Tried to save who?

STEERPIKE: Barquentine... Heard him scream... His beard and rags... Burning... no water... Beat the flames out with my bare hands, but... Panicked... caught hold of me... Caught fire... Both burning... ran to the window... Jumped in the moat... (*Clutches the Doctor's arm.*) Doctor, I couldn't hold him!

PRUNESQUALLOR: Hush! You'll tell me about it tomorrow. Sleep.

DR PRUNESQUALLOR gives him an injection. STEERPIKE falls into a restless sleep. Enter FUCHSIA, distressed.

FUCHSIA: Doctor Prune! Is he all right?

PRUNESQUALLOR: As right as rain, my dear! Rain that is, subject to certain infirmities of fire and water! Hahaha! But my dear, by all that's unwholesome, what are you doing here?

FUCHSIA: Doctor Prune... What really happened to father?

PRUNESQUALLOR: Believe me, Fuchsia, I don't know. I know he was sick... you know that as well as I do. But no one knows what happened to him, except perhaps Flay or Swelter...

FUCHSIA: Mr Flay is alive, doctor. Titus has seen him. You mustn't tell... it's a secret.

PRUNESQUALLOR: Flay? Alive! Titus? But he mustn't... you mustn't see him, Fuchsia. It will bring nothing but trouble.

FUCHSIA: But you said he might know about father.

COUNTESS: (*Appearing at the door.*) Your father is dead, Fuchsia.

FUCHSIA: Are you following me? Are you? (*Storms off.*)

PRUNESQUALLOR: My Lady, by all that's unpredictable...

COUNTESS: Hold your horses! Hold! Hold hard! You can come in now.

DR PRUNESQUALLOR's utter bewilderment is somewhat relieved when white cats swarm into the room, padding, pawing, purring around the COUNTESS.

We're... all... here...

PRUNESQUALLOR: Haha! Indeed, your Ladyship, here, as you so succinctly put it, you all are. What a party we shall have. Mew-sical chairs? Hahaha!

COUNTESS: Prunesquallor.

PRUNESQUALLOR: (*Instantly serious and attentive.*) Madam?

COUNTESS: There is mischief in the castle. Where, I do not know. But there is mischief…

PRUNESQUALLOR: Mischief? Some – bad influence?

COUNTESS: An enemy. Whether ghost or human I do not know – but an enemy – you understand?

PRUNESQUALLOR: Not a ghost, madam. Ghosts have no itch for rebellion.

COUNTESS: Rebellion? Who would dare to rebel? Who would dare? I'll break it! I'll crush its life out – not only for Titus – for Gormenghast! (*Abruptly pragmatic.*) Barquentine is dead. His son must be found and invested as Master –

PRUNESQUALLOR: He had no son, my Lady. He was training Steerpike…

COUNTESS: Steerpike? The boy who rescued us from the library?

PRUNESQUALLOR: Indeed, your Ladyship. Not content with saving two generations of the House of Groan, the young man suffered severe burns in his efforts to extinguish Barquentine. He seems to have a quite uncanny ability to appear at the scene of conflagrations. Positively infernal, hahaha!

COUNTESS: (*Stares at the sleeping STEERPIKE.*) Will he live?

PRUNESQUALLOR: God willing, my Lady – though I fear only death will heal his scars.

COUNTESS: He shall be my Master of Ritual… No change 'Squallor!

The COUNTESS sails off, unruffled and seemingly oblivious to DR PRUNESQUALLOR's disquiet.

PRUNESQUALLOR: (*Muses.*) No change, my Lady? Would that it were so…

STEERPIKE: (*Crying out in delirium.*) The old Earl... The books... burning... death owl... one... Barquentine, two... Cora and Clarice... three, four...

DR PRUNESQUALLOR eavesdrops, troubled.

And Titus Groan will make it five!

STEERPIKE's demonic laughter.

Blackout.

Act Three
The Flood

SCENE 1
The Poisoned Chalice

STEERPIKE, the new Master of Ritual, raises a ceremonial chalice. He takes out a vial of poison, pours it into the chalice, sniffs it, smiling with professional pride.
SWELTER'S GHOST appears above, bathed in a lime-green light, mournfully singing:

SWELTER: Steerpike. Steerpike. Steerpike. Steerpike...
       Skew-bald... His ruined face... white and scarlet...
       Burnt beyond repair... Eyes the colour of dried blood...
       Every word, every deed, every motive ulterior...
       Holds the Castle in the scalded palm of his hand...
       Where does he come from? What does he mean?

(*Calling down.*) Tell me Steerpike, what does it all mean?

SWELTER'S GHOST vanishes.

SCENE 2
The Earling

Distant thunder. Sporadic flashes of lightning. A CROWD of shadows. An iron bell rings. Enter FUCHSIA. STEERPIKE presents her with the chalice. They exchange furtive looks. Above: The COUNTESS appears on a rostrum decked with ritual emblems, watching with foreboding. Beside her, TITUS gazes gloomily out over his domain.

STEERPIKE: (*Ritually invoking the spirit of the Castle.*) Gormenghast!

Bells and gongs chime. TITUS descends from the rostrum to kneel and kiss the earth, performing the ritual with a weariness reminiscent of his father Sepulchrave.

(*Declaiming.*) It is written, and the writing adhered to, that the Earl of Gormenghast be invested with all due ceremony as a living symbol of the Castle. I, Steerpike, Master of Ritual, hereby declare that this Earling shall in no way violate the ancient tenets…

COUNTESS: (*Shouting down at him.*) Get on with it!

STEERPIKE: Let the Earling commence!

Bells, gongs, drums. FUCHSIA hands the chalice to TITUS. He makes to drink. THE THING suddenly springs from the shadows, snatching the chalice from his hand.
All stand rooted to the spot as THE THING dances off with the chalice. On an impulse, TITUS chases after her.

FUCHSIA: (*Makes after him.*) Titus!

COUNTESS: Titus! (*To STEERPIKE.*) Stop them!

STEERPIKE: (*Restraining her.*) Lady Fuchsia!

FUCHSIA: (*Despairing.*) Oh, Steerpike, what has he done?

STEERPIKE: (*Whispering urgently.*) Your brother has violated the Castle's most hallowed rite. You must find him. He must drink! He must complete the ceremony. Understand? (*She nods.*) Your mother will be angry if I let you go. You must appear to defy me. (*Feigns trying to hold her.*) Lady Fuchsia, I beg you!

FUCHSIA: (*Shouting for the COUNTESS's benefit.*) Let me go! (*Breaks free and runs off.*)

COUNTESS: Why? Why? (*Exits, above, shouting.*) 'Squallor! Squallor!

STEERPIKE: (*Alone, surveying his intended domain.*) Find him, Fuchsia. Make him drink. And when he has drunk, all this shall be yours. And you shall be mine. All mine.

Light fades on STEERPIKE.

SCENE 3
Death of The Thing

Isolated splashes of rain quickly turn into a torrential downpour. An abandoned part of the castle, overgrown. Enter and exit in rapid succession: THE THING, chased by TITUS, running blindly in the storm, followed by FUCHSIA, staggering through the rain on the verge of collapse.

THE THING reappears, having given them the slip. She crawls into the mouth of her cave. Inside the cave, THE THING squats like a frog, plucking feathers from a magpie. She gobbles the raw meat, tossing aside the bones. Wipes her mouth. Scratches her thigh.

TITUS appears at the entrance to the cave, watching her. She picks up the chalice she stole, staring at it from different angles, her head on one side like a bird. She drinks, guzzling greedily, the puts down the chalice and rises in a single, fluid movement, stretching with cat-like grace. She freezes, sensing danger, her eyes scanning the shadows.

TITUS enters the cave. THE THING snatches a stone and hurls it at him, backing off as he advances.

TITUS: Can't you understand? I am your friend. Your friend! I am Lord Titus. Can't you hear me? I've run away! I followed you… I've found you… So speak to me, for God's sake! Speak, can't you?

THE THING makes a silent gesture of trust. TITUS removes the chain from round his neck, showing her the Key.

Look! The Key to the Iron Gate. My mother gave it me… the Key that may not be used. But you could use it. You could unlock the Iron Gate. Here! Take it. It's yours.

He offers her the Key. THE THING leans forward, snatching at it. He catches hold of her, trying to restrain her. She struggles. He grips her tighter, pinning her down, kissing her. THE THING convulses, then goes limp. THE THING dies in TITUS's arms. He cradles her, in shock. The storm abates. Rain drips. FUCHSIA appears, crawling into the cave.

FUCHSIA: Titus!

TITUS: (*Without emotion.*) She's dead, Fuchsia.

FUCHSIA: What? Who?

TITUS: The wild girl.

FUCHSIA: The Thing? Titus, how could you? The Thing.
They say she was cursed. They say...

TITUS: I don't care! I don't care what they say. I loved her...

FUCHSIA: Don't tell me, Titus. I don't want to know. You
live your life and I'll live mine. Oh God! Is there nothing
but death and beastliness?

FLAY appears. He coughs discreetly.

TITUS: (*No emotion.*) Hullo, Mr Flay. You look wonderful and
wild...

FLAY: Ladyship says you missed your Earling... forgive me,
Lordship, but... for the Earl to miss his own Earling...

FUCHSIA: (*Retrieves the chalice.*) There's still some left. Titus...
(*Offers the chalice. He refuses it.*) Titus, you must.

TITUS: Must what?

FUCHSIA: Complete the ceremony.

TITUS: Says who? Steerpike? I've seen you, Fuchsia.

FUCHSIA: What's that supposed to mean?

TITUS: It means I don't want you to see him.

FUCHSIA: What do you know about him? Is it a crime for
him to be more brilliant than we could ever be? Is it his
fault that he's disfigured?

FLAY: (*Coughs.*) Lady Fuchsia... forgive me, but... the
ceremony... Barquentine...

FUCHSIA: Barquentine's dead, Mr Flay. Burnt to death.
Steerpike tried to save him.

FLAY: (*Agitated.*) But the Ritual… Who makes the symbols come to life? Who turns the wheels of Gormenghast?

FUCHSIA: It's all right, Mr Flay. Steerpike wasn't trained for nothing.

FLAY: Steerpike? No! No! He's no Master of Ritual! No love, Ladyship. No love for Gormenghast.

TITUS: I wish there wasn't a Master of Ritual, or a Gormenghast. I wish they'd burn the whole place down!

FLAY: (*Sharply.*) Terrible thing to say, Lordship! Terrible…

FUCHSIA: Titus. (*Offers chalice.*) Drink.

He angrily dashes the chalice to the ground. She turns away, hurt.

FLAY: (*Retrieves the chalice, sniffing it suspiciously.*) Lordship… Thing… Did she… (*Indicates chalice.*)

TITUS nods, startled out of his grief, grasping his meaning. FLAY silences him before he can say more.

(*Indicating FUCHSIA, whispering.*) No proof, Lordship… (*Muttering to himself.*) Beast… loose in the House… Must destroy it… before it… (*Sees FUCHSIA staring at him oddly.*) Ladyship… must go back… They'll be looking for you… They'll be looking for you… They'll be looking for you…

He leads them off.

SCENE 4
The Countess Wakes

Castle courtyard. Enter COUNTESS, listening intently to DR PRUNESQUALLOR.

PRUNESQUALLOR: He was delirious, mind, but he spoke quite distinctly. 'And Titus Groan will make it five.'

COUNTESS: Five what?

PRUNESQUALLOR: Exactly, my Lady, five what?

COUNTESS: Five enigmas? (*Ponders.*)
    The Earl, my husband, vanished – one…
    Swelter, the cook, vanished – two…
    Cora and Clarice, vanished – three…
    Barquentine burnt alive – four…

PRUNESQUALLOR: 'And Titus Groan will make it five!'

COUNTESS: Two fires… And the youth at both!

PRUNESQUALLOR: The youth?

COUNTESS: Steerpike!

PRUNESQUALLOR: Ah! We have the same fears.

COUNTESS: It is too early. Give him rope…

Enter TITUS and FUCHSIA, shamefaced. She surveys them in silence.

Fuchsia, go to your room. Lock your door. 'Squallor…

PRUNESQUALLOR: Come my dear. (*Leads FUCHSIA off.*)
What a storm! And worse to come, by all that's torrential, there surely is!

The COUNTESS circles TITUS, scrutinising him closely. She slaps his face.

COUNTESS: You are the last of the line. You are
Gormenghast.

TITUS: (*No emotion.*) No change, mother.

COUNTESS: (*Gripping his arm, suddenly maternal.*) Oh, Titus!
(*Restraining herself, coldly.*) Go to your room

Exit TITUS. During her soliloquy, the COUNTESS is dressed in battle-armour by her retainers.

By the black tap-root of the Castle, if my fear is
  founded…
The oldest stones will sicken and spew,
The towers be gorged with his blood,
His liver and heart for the cats to chew

His entrails to rot in the mud.
And the carrion crow flap down from the sky
To pluck the brains from the hollow eyes
Of his skull on a spike on Traitor's Gate…

Defiantly shaking her spear at an unseen enemy.

Beware!

The Warrior COUNTESS storms off.

SCENE 5
Fuchsia Betrayed

FUCHSIA sneaks out of her room, goes off down a corridor. FLAY silently stalks her, his knees bandaged. FUCHSIA reappears in a shadowy corridor. Glancing furtively about her, she taps on a door. No answer. She paces nervously, knocks again.

FLAY: (*Voice from the shadows.*) Be careful, my Lady…

FUCHSIA: (*Startled, terrified, hammering on the door.*) Steerpike! Steerpike! Let me in! Steerpike!

STEERPIKE appears, forcing his hand over her mouth and pushing her roughly through the door.

STEERPIKE: (*Hissing in the dark.*) Fool!

STEERPIKE bundles FUCHSIA into the room, locking the door. FUCHSIA breaks free and stares at him coldly – hurt, yet proud, resentful.

FUCHSIA: Let me out of here.

STEERPIKE: (*Realising his mistake, buries his face in his hands, watching her through the slits in his fingers.*) Fuchsia… What can I say? There is no excuse for what I did, but… at least let me try to explain. Do you know what would happen to you if we were caught, a daughter of the line consorting with a commoner? It's too awful to think about. That's why our meetings must be so secret…

FUCHSIA: It's too late. Everything's changed. I don't feel the same any more.

STEERPIKE: But tonight, you misjudged the time. Tonight, of all nights, when your mother's men were following...

FUCHSIA: (*Startled.*) My mother?

STEERPIKE: There was no time to be lost. A moment later and your screaming would have led them to this door. Put yourself in my place. I had no time to be polite. My only thought was to save you. Can't you see? I love you, Fuchsia. I called you 'fool' – yes 'fool' – out of love for you – and then... and now, it all seems so unbelievable, and I'm so ashamed... I don't even know if I can show you the present I bought you. (*Sighs, relenting.*) Oh, come on then, Satan... Come on my wicked boy!

He opens a door to reveal a tame monkey.
FUCHSIA shakes her head wearily.

You don't like Satan?

FUCHSIA: 'Satan'?

STEERPIKE: Your monkey. I thought he would please you. I chose him myself.

FUCHSIA: I don't know. I don't know! I don't know, I tell you!

STEERPIKE: Fuchsia... Try to understand...

FUCHSIA: I will never understand. It's no good, however much you talk. I may've been wrong. I don't know. I want to go now.

STEERPIKE: Of course. But promise you'll meet me one last time. Tomorrow night.

FUCHSIA: I don't know. I don't know!

STEERPIKE: If you don't I'll –

FUCHSIA: I don't know! But – I suppose so. O God, I suppose so.

STEERPIKE: Thank you, my dear, sweet Fuchsia. (*Kisses her, very gently.*)

FUCHSIA: Steerpike… I think you're going soft.

STEERPIKE: Tomorrow night, then.

He leads her to the door and off.

(*Alone.*) So? Won't have us, won't she? Well, my precious… We'll have her, tomorrow night and no mistake. We'll have her. We'll have her. We'll have her! Then… Then we take care of him!

SCENE 6
Doctor Prune To The Rescue

The corridor. STEERPIKE opens the door, emerges and strides briskly off, stalked by FLAY. FUCHSIA comes out. Alone, she has lost the poise she maintained with STEERPIKE. She wanders up and down the corridor disorientated. Enter DR PRUNESQUALLOR.

PRUNESQUALLOR: Fuchsia! (*Greeting her with forced jollity.*) My dear child, by all that's synchronic, that I should happen to be… Fuchsia? What is it child?

FUCHSIA: Oh Doctor Prune… (*Breaks down, sobbing.*)

PRUNESQUALLOR: There, there… what is it? Can it be love I spy in your pretty eye? Ah, love, that's dangerous enough, but love that is forbidden, by all paths perilous… Do you want to tell me about it, my dear?

FUCHSIA: (*Pulls herself together.*) You mustn't say you saw me here. You won't, will you? Promise? (*Harkening to the sound of footsteps, clutching him.*) Doctor Prune, help me!

PRUNESQUALLOR: Don't worry, my dear. I'll think of something.

Enter TITUS, running.

TITUS: Doctor Prune… Oh! Hullo Fuchsia. Doctor Prune, quick! Flay says you're to come immediately.

PRUNESQUALLOR: Flay?

TITUS: He's returned from exile – but to save Fuchsia and me and the Laws – but come quickly, doctor! (*Aside.*) We're tracking Steerpike. Flay wants you as a witness.

PRUNESQUALLOR: Witness? Haha! I'm flattered. Hahaha! (*Coughs.*) Fuchsia, my dear, I want you to go straight to your room and lock the door. And as soon as I'm done with Mr Flay you and I will have a good long talk. What do you say?

FUCHSIA walks off without saying a word.

TITUS: This way, Doctor Prune! There's no time to lose! Flay said he'd chalk us a trail… He knows all the secret passages…

TITUS hurries DR PRUNESQUALLOR off.
FUCHSIA reappears, following them. Distant thunder. Flashes of lightning.

SCENE 7

Stalking Steerpike

Chase sequence. STEERPIKE glides down corridors and twisting stone lanes, silently stalked by FLAY, who chalks a trail on the floor. TITUS and DR PRUNESQUALLOR follow the trail, and are in turn shadowed by FUCHSIA.
They enter a deserted province of Gormenghast, a place abandoned, hollow, empty. They spy FLAY, lurking at the edge of an open square. He silently gestures for them to join him. Together they watch as: STEERPIKE, on the far side of the square, plays a macabre jig on his sword-stick.

PRUNESQUALLOR: (*Whispers.*) Is there nothing he can't do? By all that's versatile, he frightens me!

FLAY hushes him as STEERPIKE stops playing. He glides away into a labyrinth of passageways. They follow. FUCHSIA follows them.

SCENE 8
Evil Unmasked

STEERPIKE arrives at his destination. He unbolts and unlocks a rusty iron door, opening a cell to reveal the skeletons of CORA and CLARICE, wearing the same dresses and strings of pearls, seated side by side. FLAY, TITUS and DR PRUNESQUALLOR hide, watching. FUCHSIA sneaks up behind them, unnoticed.

STEERPIKE: Your Ladyships... (*Bows.*) How do you like your thrones? All yours now, the power and the glory... Such dainty little bones. (*Cackles.*) Shall we bleach 'em, my dears? Shall we? Slosh 'em in moonlight? (*Carries the skeletons out onto the terrace.*) There! Sing your little hearts out, my lovelies. No one's listening. We'll make 'em turn, my dears, and what a turn – for them and the worms that nibble 'em! What's the matter, don't you want to sing? And what do you propose to do in this batter? I've seen you looking at me with your insolent animal eyes. You're looking at me now! Tell me, ladies, what does it all mean?

FLAY moves to arrest him. His knee-joints crack, alerting STEERPIKE, who draws the sword from his stick.

PRUNESQUALLOR: Drop your sword! You are under arrest.

STEERPIKE lunges at FLAY, running him through with his sword, and dashes off. FLAY collapses in TITUS's arms.

TITUS: Flay! Mr Flay...

FLAY: Lordship... Tell your mother... what you saw...

TITUS: Mr Flay... Did he... kill my father?

FLAY: Field of Stones... Owls... (*Dies.*)

DR PRUNESQUALLOR closes FLAY's eyes.
Seeing FUCHSIA, TITUS goes to her.

TITUS: He's dead, Fuchsia.

FUCHSIA: Who?

TITUS: Flay, of course!

FUCHSIA: Titus... I love you, Titus, but I can't feel anything and I don't want to. I've felt too much. I'm sick of feelings. I've gone dead. Even you are dead to me.

PRUNESQUALLOR: Fuchsia! My dear child, this is no place for you.

FUCHSIA: It's all right, doctor, I'm going.

TITUS: Going where?

FUCHSIA: To the Field of Stones. I have to speak to father.

FUCHSIA wanders off distractedly.

TITUS: Take care of her, doctor. I'm going after Steerpike.

PRUNESQUALLOR: But, my Lord, by all that's unconstitutional...

TITUS: My sister! For God's sake, doctor, attend to your patient!

They rush off in opposite directions.

PRUNESQUALLOR: (*Calling querulously, off.*) Fuchsia! Fuchsia!

Demented music.

SCENE 9

Fuchsia's Suicide

FUCHSIA appears on the roof, gazing down at the dizzying drop. Lightning flashes. Owls hoot.
A pair of huge, glowing, saucer-shaped eyes light up.

FUCHSIA: Father? Oh, father!

FUCHSIA smiles beatifically, reaching out, gracefully spreading her arms and arching her body like a diver. She plunges to her death. Lightning flashes. Crash of thunder.

SCENE 10
The Flood

Thunder. Lightning. Deluge. Torrential rain hisses and hammers on the roof and walls. A huge silk is unfurled to create the effect of water pouring in through doors and windows to flood the ground floor of the castle.
Pandemonium. Servants battle to salvage vital provisions – hauling furniture and valuables up stairways to save them from the rising flood.
Enter the COUNTESS, alert, decisive, formidable. She immediately establishes order amidst the confusion, interviewing a succession of servants.

COUNTESS: Well?

SERVANT 1: It's true, your Ladyship. The lower storeys are flooded. They are building boats and launching them out of windows.

COUNTESS: Inform them their craft may be requisitioned in emergency. Is the leader of the Heavy Rescue here?

SERVANT 2: Yes, your Ladyship.

COUNTESS: Rest your men.

SERVANT 2: Yes, your Ladyship. They need it.

COUNTESS: We all need it. What of it? You have your list? Have the section leaders made their working copies? Good! Next!

SERVANT 3: Your Ladyship! The waters are still rising. We see no break in the storm.

COUNTESS: Good!

All turn to stare at the COUNTESS, puzzled.

In six hours' time the flood will be at our feet. The night cannot be spent on this level. The Chequered Stairway is the widest. You have my orders of priority: livestock, carcasses, corn?

SERVANT 3: Yes, my Lady.

COUNTESS: Are the cats comfortable?

SERVANT 3: They have the run of the twelve blue attics.

COUNTESS: Ah! Then... Then, gentlemen, we shall begin.
The rising water draws us all together, is that not so,
gentlemen? With every hour less rooms are tenable.
We are driven up, are we not, into a confine. Tell me
gentlemen, can traitors live on thin air? Can they chew
clouds, or swallow the thunder and fill their bellies with
lightning? (*SERVANTS shake their heads, perplexed.*) Great
hell, he is no merman! He has no tail or fins. No... He is
like us, gentlemen! Are the sentries posted? The kitchen
guarded? No doubt the beast must feed.

CHORUS: No change!

COUNTESS: All those not involved in the Heavy Rescue
shall be issued with weapons and torches and given their
orders of search. Not a cranny unscoured! Not a drain
unprobed!

The COUNTESS strides off, leading her retinue.
A search-party of ARMED GUARDS with torches wades
through flooded chambers. Thwack of a catapult. A GUARD
falls face down in the water. STEERPIKE wades out to plunder
the floating corpse. He climbs up the wall, ducking through a
window. TITUS emerges from an alcove, climbs up the wall and
disappears through the window after him.

SCENE 11
The Hunt

A landing. Enter the COUNTESS, attended by SERVANTS
holding a map.

COUNTESS: Cordons of hand-picked guards converging
inwards to the centre of each district... Here! Here! Here!
All craft will patrol the Headstones night and day. Search
parties will muster at Dogshead. Is my boat prepared?

SERVANT 1: This way, your Ladyship... My Lady, we must cast off without delay. The flood has already breached the –

COUNTESS: Cats?

SERVANT 2: Safe!

They lead her down to a boat moored in the flooded stairwell.

COUNTESS: And the books of the Law?

SERVANT 1: Safe!

COUNTESS: Tell the Professors to elect a new Master of Ritual. The Ceremonies shall proceed as usual.

SERVANTS: No change!

COUNTESS: There is no change.

They help her into the boat. TITUS bursts in, on the verge of collapse, bruised and scratched, his clothes sodden and torn, hair matted with grime.

TITUS: Mother!

COUNTESS: What is it?

TITUS: I've seen him!

COUNTESS: Who?

TITUS: Steerpike!

COUNTESS: Where?

TITUS: On the roof... In the Field of Stones...

COUNTESS: (*Stiffens.*) No... Why should I believe you?

TITUS: It's true! I followed him. I can take you there. In the North Wing the waters are lapping at the roof.

COUNTESS: Did he see you?

TITUS: No.

COUNTESS: Sure?

TITUS: Yes

COUNTESS: Then we have him! (*To SERVANTS.*) Summon the Search Captains! The district will be ringed at once! On every level! (*SERVANTS run off. To TITUS.*) Get in! You have done well. Gormenghast will be avenged. The castle's heart is sound. You have surprised me.

TITUS: I didn't do it for Gormenghast.

COUNTESS: No?

TITUS: No, mother.

COUNTESS: Then for whom? For what?

TITUS: I have my own reasons.

COUNTESS: (*Menacingly.*) What... reasons?

TITUS: (*Defiantly.*) I'll tell you! I'll tell you! He hurt Fuchsia. He killed Flay. He tried to kill me, only The Thing got it instead. I don't care if it's rebellion against the Stones! What do I care if the Castle's heart is sound? Anybody can be sound if they're always doing what they're told. Can't you see? He killed Flay. He hurt my sister. Isn't that enough? To hell with Gormenghast!

A terrible silence. DR PRUNESQUALLOR appears, distraught. He waits, bowed and trembling, for permission to speak.

COUNTESS: Well, what is it, man? Speak!

PRUNESQUALLOR: My Lady... by all that's unspeakable...

COUNTESS: No! Not Fuchsia! For God's sake, 'Squallor, where is she?

PRUNESQUALLOR: No one knows, my Lady. She's been missing since the night of the storm. I should never have left her...

TITUS: The Field of Stones! Oh God, mother, we must find him – before he finds Fuchsia. Mother!

He startles the COUNTESS from her nightmare, helping her and DR PRUNESQUALLOR into the boat with the GUARDS.

COUNTESS: Cast off!

The ENSEMBLE form the 'boat' – setting sail for the Field of Stones. The roof of the Castle rises like an island above the floodwater lake.

GUARD: Careful, my Lady. We've lost thirty men already.

COUNTESS: What do I care if you lose thirty thousand? The Stones must be avenged!

SCENE 12
Steerpike's Death

The 'boat' dissolves, reforming on the upper level. Above: the COUNTESS, TITUS and GUARDS scan the waters. Alerted by a splash, they see STEERPIKE swimming below.

GUARD: (*Pointing.*) There! In the water!

COUNTESS: Well? What are you waiting for? Kill the beast!

TITUS: (*Draws his knife.*) I'll kill him myself!

COUNTESS: No! By the blood of love. Hold the boy!

PRUNESQUALLOR: (*Grips TITUS.*) Easy, my Lord...

TITUS: (*Struggles.*) Let me go! Do you know who I am? Let go!

TITUS wrenches free and dives into the water.

COUNTESS: Titus!

TITUS dives down into the murky depths, his knife poised to stab. He recoils in horror from the limp, sodden corpse of FUCHSIA. He drags her body to the surface, choking and spluttering, passing her up to the COUNTESS, who is now on the roof.

No... (*Screams.*) No!!!

TITUS takes a deep breath and plunges back down to where STEERPIKE lurks, holding his breath. They fight, stabbing with long knives, their movements impeded by the mass of water.

TITUS stabs STEERPIKE in the belly, the thrust lifting him out of the water. STEERPIKE howls, dies.
Above: the COUNTESS tenderly cradles the dead FUCHSIA.
Below: TITUS lays STEERPIKE's corpse on the ground, like an offering to his mother.

(*Distractedly.*) Burn it!

Sound of crackling flames as STEERPIKE's corpse is enveloped in red light. A piercing inhuman scream, then silence.

SCENE 13

Titus Alone

A long silence. TITUS stands up awkwardly.

TITUS: Mother… (*Pause.*) Mother. I'm going… (*Long pause.*) Goodbye.

COUNTESS: Going where?

TITUS: Away. I'm leaving Gormenghast. I can't explain. I have to go. Goodbye, mother…

TITUS takes the Key from his neck, unlocks the Iron Gate and walks out through it, towards the auditorium. The jagged silhouette of Gormenghast Castle recedes behind him. A white silk is slowly raised, separating him from the Castle. Above, in the distance, his family and friends appear on the ramparts: SIREN VOICES, GHOSTS, PHANTOMS.

CHORUS: To north, south, east and west, all landmarks gone. Where is he now, Titus the Abdicator?

TITUS: (*Calling out.*) Can you hear me?

COUNTESS: My son?

TITUS: Where are you, mother? Where are you?

CHORUS: Where are you? Where are you? Where?

COUNTESS: Where I always am.

TITUS: At your high window, mother, aswarm with birds?

COUNTESS: Where else?

CHORUS: The birds are perched upon her head like leaves...
And the cats like a white river...

COUNTESS: The cats are loyal in a traitor's world.

CHORUS: Gone the labyrinth that fed his dreams...
Gone ritual, his marrow and his bone...

FLAY: Why d'you do it, Lordship? Why d'you run away?

PRUNESQUALLOR: My dear Titus, by all that abdicates,
you take the cake.

CHORUS: Why did you do it? Why did you? Why?

COUNTESS: Your father, your sister... and now you...

FUCHSIA: Titus! Remember? My black hair in my eyes...

TITUS: I couldn't wait, Fuchsia. The Thing was...

FLAY: The owls are on their way... From Gormenghast...
The owls... The owls... The little ravenous owls...

TITUS: Dig a great pit for them... Sing to them...

CHORUS: Torn world of towers... Gone... Gone the grey
lichen...
Gone the black ivy... Gone childhood... Gone...

TITUS: Forgive me... I have to go... Go...

COUNTESS: There is nowhere to go. Not a road, not a track,
but will lead you home. You will only tread a circle, Titus
Groan. Everything returns... to Gormenghast...

*The white silk rises, concealing the COUNTESS and
Gormenghast Castle, leaving TITUS alone in the spotlight.*

Fade to black.

The End

www.ingramcontent.com/pod-product-compliance
Ingram Content Group UK Ltd.
Pitfield, Milton Keynes, MK11 3LW, UK
UKHW020728280225
455688UK00012B/558